2nd Grade Spy Kids and the Missing Skateboard

By

JORDAN D. GILLIAM

Illustrations Inspired by ALDO AVALOS

Cover Design/Colorization: AFFORDABLE PUBLISHING COMPANY, San Diego, CA.

Published in the United States by REGS Books, a division of Regina Mixon Enterprises, California.

2nd Grade Spy Kids and the Missing Skateboard is a registered trademark of REGS Books Publishing.

www.regsbooks.org

www.reginamixonenterprises.org

Educators and librarians, for a variety of teaching tools, visit us at www.regsbooks.org

Library of Congress Control Number: In-Process

ISBN: 978-0-9820699-9-8
Printed in the United States of America

Hi! My name is Jordan. I am 8 years old.

Writing stops me from being bored. Writing is easy to do.

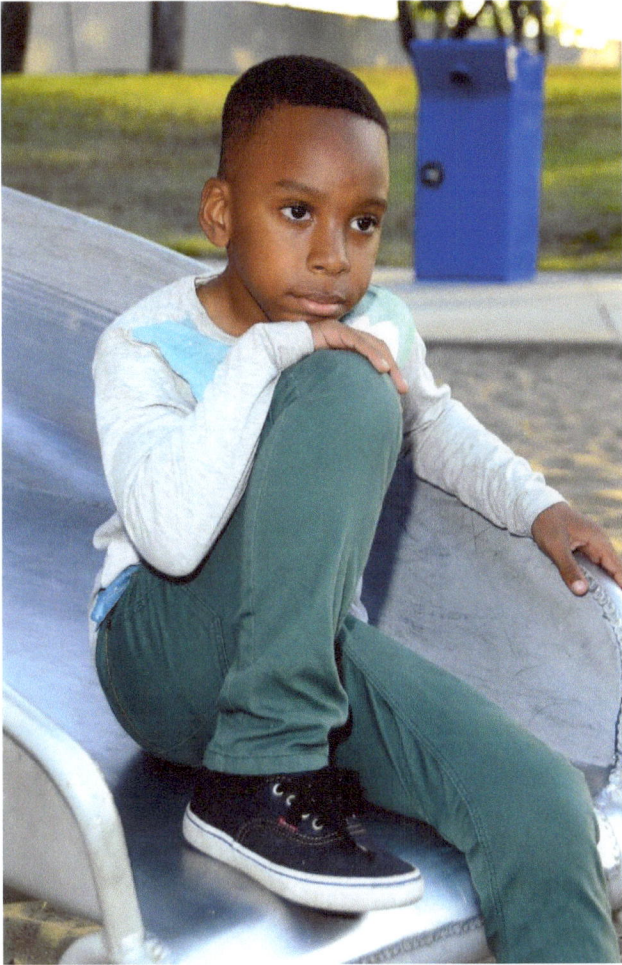

Just stop and think then begin to write.

I love to read
and write. That is
why I wrote this
book for you.

It was a sunny day and Jordan, Jeremy, and Celeste were playing outside. Jordan said, "I'll be right back. I'm going to get my skateboard." But when he looked he couldn't see it.

Jordan went back outside and told his friends the bad news. So they looked all over the house.

Then Celeste said, "I found a wheel to the skateboard". And then they saw a trail of skateboard wheels that leads to an abandoned subway station and when they got down there they saw a man with a bag of skateboards.

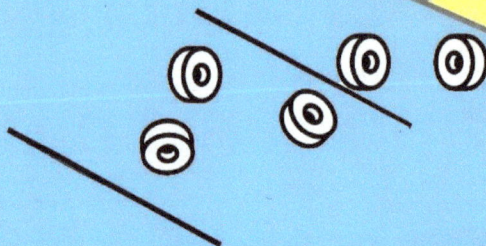

The man with the skateboards was using the wheels to see if they fit his skateboards. And he tried all the wheels that he had but they didn't fit. Then the kids saw him coming so they ducked down and waited for him to leave.

And then, the man got into his car and drove away.

The kids called a taxi and told him to follow the man's car. The man's car stopped in front of a skateboard shop. He went in and when he came out he had two bags full of skateboards and the sirens were ringing.

Jordan, Jeremy and Celeste did not know that the man had stolen the skateboards but they later found out that he had.

The man got back into his car and drove back to the subway station. He tried some more wheels to see if they fit his skateboard.

SUBWA

A pair of wheels that he had gotten from the skateboard shop fit.

He set a fire and was about to put the skateboards in the fire because he didn't need them.

The kids jumped out of the bushes and told him not to throw the skateboards in the fire. He was surprised to see the kids.

The man's face turned red as he was embarrassed. He had been caught.

Then the man asked why can't I throw them in the fire? "Because you can still fix them and give them back to the kids that you stole them from" said Jeremy.

The man had stolen lots of skateboards from the shop and other kids

The man fixed the skateboards and gave them back to the kids and Jordan got his skateboard back. You see, the man had stolen his skateboard too.

Jordan, Jeremy, and Celeste were very happy. They played together. Jordan let Jeremy and Celeste play on his skateboard. They were so happy!

The case of the missing skateboard was solved

THE END

Now you write!

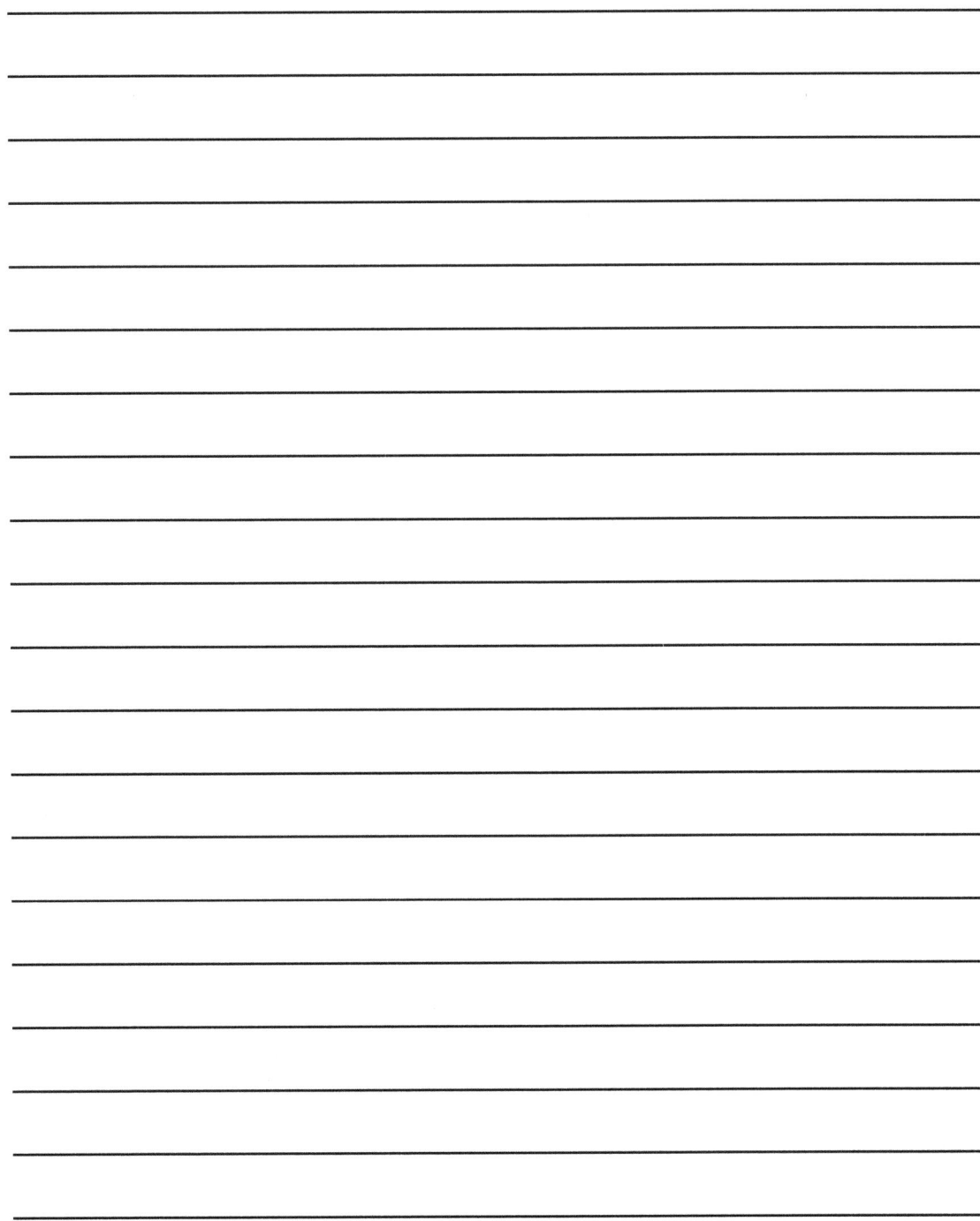

GOOD JOB!

www.ingramcontent.com/pod-product-compliance
Lightning Source LLC
Chambersburg PA
CBHW041308310326
41914CB00113B/1489